THEATRE UNCUT

THEATRE UNCUT

New short plays by Clara Brennan, David Greig, Dennis Kelly, Lucy Kirkwood, Laura Lomas, Anders Lustgarten, Mark Ravenhill and Jack Thorne, in response to the countrywide spending cuts

OBERON BOOKS
LONDON

WWW.OBERONBOOKS.COM

This collection first published in 2011 by Oberon Books Ltd
521 Caledonian Road, London N7 9RH
Tel: +44 (0) 20 7607 3637 / Fax: +44 (0) 20 7607 3629
e-mail: info@oberonbooks.com
www.oberonbooks.com

A catalogue record for this book is available from the British
Library.

ISBN: 978-1-84943-063-0

Cover image: Nina Feldman.

Printed in Great Britain by CPI Antony Rowe, Chippenham.

Contents

INTRODUCTION

On March 19th 2011 eighty-nine groups across the UK, the USA and Germany, took these plays and made them their own. In a unique theatrical event, nearly a thousand people nationwide came together to use theatre to make a stand, to simultaneously raise their voices in a theatrical protest that said no to the spending cuts announced by the Coalition government in October 2010. In theatres, in bars, in universities, in kitchens, living-rooms and bedrooms; these plays were performed, read aloud, read privately, discussed, thought about and used as a catalyst to action. Theatre Uncut had begun.

Theatre Uncut has been extraordinary in many ways. Growing above and beyond all expectation, capturing the imaginations of theatre-makers up and down the country, Theatre Uncut's overriding ethos is participation and collaboration. From the extraordinary support of Mark Ravenhill and David Greig, without whom the project would never have happened, to the help of Casarotto, The Southwark Playhouse, Prospero PR, our wonderful casts and crews, our incredible Creative Producer Libby Brodie, the Reclaim Production and Meeting Point Production teams and other contributors too numerous to name check: Theatre Uncut proves that collaboration is the key to creating extraordinary theatre.

Theatre Uncut is of course a politically motivated collective, which exists entirely because groups across the country took part and stood in solidarity. I believe very strongly that we are at a crisis point, both in the finer detail of how and where the cuts manifest themselves, but also in the move towards a society that is more selfish, more greedy, and less altruistic than ever. What theatre does best is explore the society around it, existing in the crossover between the ephemeral and the retrospective. These plays do that magnificently: from Jack Thorne and Dennis Kelly's blistering and hilarious summation of pedagogy dressed as politics, to Mark Ravenhill and Lucy Kirkwood's exploration of the birth of the welfare state, to David Greig's *Fragile*, a visceral exploration of a beleaguered mental health care system, Laura

Lomas' beautiful allegory for the heart of the nation, Anders Lustgarten's hard-hitting call to arms and Clara Brennan's emotional and personal portrayal of a mother of a disabled girl in a residential care unit. These plays are quality explorations of the issues at hand. They stand them up and make them real. They use theatre's lifeblood, empathy, to show what these cuts mean and force us to address the cuts on an emotional and intuitive level.

So what next for Theatre Uncut? How can we continue to make ourselves heard? I hope that this volume will play a major role in the future life of Theatre Uncut. These plays need to be read, performed and discussed. We need to continue to use theatre to protest against these changes: changes that unfairly target the poorest sector of society, rest most heavily on the young, hit women where it hurts and take support away from the vulnerable. We need to continue to use the medium we love to fight for a society that doesn't cut essential welfare payments and the disability mobility allowance before it raises taxes on banking profits. We need to say no. This volume ensures Theatre Uncut will continue to provoke thought. These plays should be read as they were meant: as part of a movement that began on March 19th, a movement made up of hundreds of theatre-makers joining voices. A movement that I am ceaselessly proud to be part of and am delighted to see continue.

Hannah Price, April 2011

Theatre Uncut

THEATRE UNCUT's flagship London production was at Southwark Playhouse from 16th–19th March 2011. On March 19th eighty-nine groups nationwide (with 6 additional groups internationally) performed the plays as part of a theatrical uprising in protest against the spending cuts announced by the Coalition government on October 20th 2010.

Produced by Reclaim Productions
and Meeting Point Productions

Artistic Director
Hannah Price

Creative Producer
Libby Brodie for Meeting Point Productions

Open Heart Surgery by Laura Lomas
Directed by Blanche McIntyre

Lisa – Kate O'Flynn
Danny – Kett Turton

Things That Make No Sense by Dennis Kelly
Directed by Cressida Brown

A – Matthew Pearson
G – Julian Stolzenberg
B – Ruth Everett

The Fat Man written and performed by Anders Lustgarten
from an original idea by Anders Lustgarten and Simon Stephens

Fragile by David Greig
Directed by Hannah Price

Jack – Syrus Lowe

Whiff Whaff by Jack Thorne
Directed by Katie McAleese

Nigel – Nick Caldecott
Julie – Melissa Woodbridge

Housekeeping by Lucy Kirkwood
Directed by Lucy Morrison

Coal – Zawe Ashton
Joan – Ashley McGuire
Mrs Dean – Marlene Sidaway

A Bigger Banner by Mark Ravenhill
Directed by Hannah Price

Shona – Susan Wokoma
Raquel – Jo Miller
Marge – Emily Taaffe
Fred – Gunnar Cauthery

Hi Vis by Clara Brennan
Directed by Amy Hodge

Linda – Lisa Palfrey

Production Team
Production Designer – Carla Goodman
Lighting Designer – Catherine Webb
Production Manager – Ruth Parry
Sound Designer – Steve Brown
Stage Management – Amy Jewell, Kirsten Turner

For Reclaim Ltd
Assistant Producers – Nina Feldman & Anna Perkins
Assistant Producer Participation Events – Chrissy Jay

Publicity
Elin Morgan at Prospero (www.prosperoarts.co.uk)

**All profits from tickets sales
were donated to the Child Poverty Action Group**

The Writers

Clara Brennan's plays include *Rain* as part of *Lough/Rain* at the Edinburgh Festival Underbelly and Theatre Royal York, *The Curator* at One Night Stand, Soho Theatre, *Portmanteau* with The Miniaturists at The Arcola Theatre and Bike Shed Theatre, Exeter. *Rain* is currently being made into a short film with Reclaim Productions. Clara's most recent play *Bud Take The Wheel, I Feel A Song Coming On* was critically acclaimed at the Underbelly, Edinburgh Fringe Festival in 2010, and is published by Oberon. She is currently under commission to The Drum and Theatre Royal Plymouth.

Since **David Greig's** first main stage production *Europe* at The Traverse in 1996, his plays have been produced by most of the major theatre companies in the UK. His plays have also been translated and produced throughout Europe, the USA and Canada, Brazil, Australia and Japan. From 2005 to 2007 he was the first dramaturg of the National Theatre of Scotland. Plays include: *Monster In The Hall, Dunsinane, Midsummer, Kyoto, Brewers Fayre, Being Norwegian* (Oran Mor), *Damascus* (The Traverse Theatre), *Yellow Moon* (TAG Theatre Co. – TMA Best Play For Children and Young People, 2008 Brian Way Award), *Pyrenees* (Paines Plough, Tron Theatre), *The American Pilot* (The Royal Shakespeare Company, Stratford and London), *San Diego* (Edinburgh International Festival, Tron Theatre – Best New Play, Tron Theatre Awards, Herald Angel), *Outlying Islands* (Traverse Theatre, The Royal Court – Scotsman Fringe First, Herald Angel, Best New Play, Scottish Critics Awards), *Not About Pomegranates* (Al Kasaba Theatre, Ramallah, Palestine), *The Speculator* (Edinburgh International Festival, Grec Festival, Barcelona, Traverse Theatre), *Caledonia Dreaming* (7.84 Theatre Company – Herald Archangel), *The Cosmonaut's Last Message To The Woman He Once Loved In The Former Soviet Union* (Paines Plough, Tron Theatre – John Whiting Award), *Victoria* (RSC), *The Architect* (Traverse Theatre), *Europe* (Traverse Theatre), and *Stalinland* (Citizens Theatre).

Dennis Kelly is an internationally acclaimed playwright. Stage plays include *Debris* (Theatre503 and Battersea Arts Centre, 2003 & 2004); *Osama the Hero* (Paines Plough and Hampstead Theatre 2004 & 2005; winner of the Meyer Whitworth Award 2006); *After the End* (Paines Plough, Traverse Theatre, Bush Theatre, UK and international tour, 2005); *Love and Money* (Young Vic Theatre and Manchester Royal Exchange, 2006); *Taking Care of Baby* (Hampstead Theatre and Birmingham Repertory Theatre, 2006; winner of the John Whiting Award 2007); *DNA* (NT Connections, National Theatre, 2007-8); *Orphans* (Paines Plough, Traverse Theatre, Soho Theatre and Birmingham Rep, 2009; winner of a Fringe First and Herald Angel Award 2009) and *The Gods Weep* (Royal Shakespeare Company and Hampstead Theatre). In 2009 Dennis was voted Best Foreign Playwright 2009 by Theatre Heute, Germany. Work for radio includes *The Colony* (BBC Radio 3, 2004; Prix Europa Award – Best European Radio Drama and Radio & Music Award – Scripting for Broadcast 2004) and *12 Shares* (BBC Radio 4, 2005). Dennis co-wrote the award winning comedy series *Pulling* (Silver River and BBC 3, 2006-09) and wrote the book for *Matilda, the Musical* (Royal Shakespeare Company, 2010).

In 2007, **Lucy Kirkwood** graduated with a degree in English Literature from the University of Edinburgh, whilst there she wrote her first full-length stage play, *Grady Hot Potato*. Lucy's next play, *Guns or Butter* was produced at the Terror 2007 Festival at the Union Theatre, London and was subsequently broadcast by BBC Radio. In 2008 Lucy's play, *Tinderbox*, was produced by the Bush Theatre and in the same year *Hedda*, her adaptation of Ibsen's *Hedda Gabler* was produced by the Gate Theatre, London to wide critical acclaim. Lucy's play *Psychogeography* was produced at the Union Theatre's Terror 2009 Festival. Her stage adaptation of *Beauty and the Beast* co-devised and directed by Katie Mitchell was performed at the National Theatre in 2010/11. In the autumn of 2009 Lucy's play *it felt empty when the heart went at first but it is alright now* was produced by Clean Break Theatre Co. at the Arcola Theatre. The play, which received stunning reviews, was nominated for an Evening Standard Award – Best Newcomer and made Lucy joint winner of the John Whiting Award 2010. Lucy is currently under commission to Headlong Theatre Company and MTC in New York. Her play *The Small Hours* (co-written with Ed Hime) opened at the Hampstead Theatre in January 2011. Lucy has written for *Skins* (Company Pictures) and is developing an original TV series for Kudos and a new screenplay for Film4/ Ruby Films.

In 2009 **Laura Lomas** was one of six writers selected for the Paines Plough/Channel 4 Future Perfect scheme. Her plays include *Some Machine* (Paines Plough and Rose Bruford, Unicorn Theatre 2010); *The Island* (Nottingham Playhouse – Roundabout/Det Norske Oslo 2009); *Us Like Gods* (Hampstead Theatre, Heat and Light 2009); *Gypsy Girl* (Paines Plough at Soho Theatre, 2009); *10,000 Meters Deep* (Oran Mor, Glasgow/ Paines Plough 2009); *Traces* (Latitude Festival, Paines Plough, 2009); *Wasteland* (New Perspectives Theatre Co/Derby Live, 2009). Her radio plays include *Lucy Island* (BBC Radio 3, The Wire) and *Siren* (BBC Radio 3, The Verb).

Laura has recently written a short film for Coming Up (Channel 4 and Touchpaper) and is developing a project for Great Meadow Productions. She is currently on attachment at the National Theatre Studio.

Anders Lustgarten is a political activist and playwright and thus manages to earn nothing from two jobs. Both jobs involve asking difficult questions about politics and people. He has been arrested on four continents. His mum doesn't know this. His last play, *A Day at the Racists*, about the BNP but mainly about New Labour's betrayal of the working class, won the Catherine Johnson Award. His next play is about China's move from Maoism to market.

Mark Ravenhill is an internationally acclaimed playwright whose first full-length play, *Shopping and Fucking*, opened at the Royal Court Theatre Upstairs in 1996. His other works include *Faust is Dead* (ATC, UK tour, 1997); *Sleeping Around*, a joint venture with three other writers (Salisbury Playhouse, 1998); *Handbag* (Lyric Hammersmith Studio, 1998); *Some Explicit Polaroids* (Theatre Royal, Bury St Edmunds, 1999); *Mother Clap's Molly House* (National Theatre, 2001); *Totally Over You* (National Theatre, 2003); *Product* (Traverse Theatre, Edinburgh, 2005); *The Cut* (Donmar Warehouse, London, 2006); *Citizenship* (National Theatre, 2006); *pool (no water)* (Lyric Hammersmith, 2006); *Shoot/Get Treasure/Repeat* (Edinburgh Festival, 2007); *Over There* (Royal Court/Schaubühne, Berlin, 2009); *A Life in Three Acts* co-written and performed with Bette Bourne (Traverse Theatre, Edinburgh/Konninklijke Schouwburg, The Hague/ Soho Theatre, London, 2009 and St Ann's Warehouse, New York, 2010); *Nation* adapted from the Terry Pratchett novel (National Theatre, 2009); and has written the libretto for *Ten Plagues*, a new opera for Marc Almond. Mark is currently under commission to Headlong Theatre.

Jack Thorne's plays for stage include *2nd May 1997* (Bush Theatre), *When You Cure Me* (Bush Theatre), *Stacy* (Arcola and Trafalgar Studios), *Fanny and Faggot* (Finborough and Trafalgar Studios); *Burying Your Brother In The Pavement* (NT Connections) and *Bunny* (Nabokov Theatre) which won a Fringe First at the 2010 Edinburgh Festival. His work for television includes *Skins, Shameless, Cast-Offs* (co-written with Tony Roche and Alex Bulmer, nominated for the Royal Television Society's Best Drama Series 2010), *This Is England '86* (Channel 4, co-written with Shane Meadows, winner South Bank Show Best TV Drama, winner Royal Television Society's Best Writer – Drama 2011). He adapted *When You Cure Me* for radio (Radio 3) and further radio plays include *Left At The Angel* (Radio 4, nominated for the Imison Award 2008), *The Hunchback of Notre Dame* (adaptation with Alex Bulmer, Radio 4) and *People Snogging In Public Places* (Radio 3, Sony Radio Academy Award Winner 2010). His first feature film *The Scouting Book For Boys* (Celador and Film Four) won Jack the Star of London Best Newcomer award at the London Film Festival 2009.

OPEN HEART SURGERY

BY LAURA LOMAS

Characters

LISA

Lights up. LISA, a young woman, is sat on a chair next to an empty hospital bed. A moment. She looks at us.

LISA: They'll be back soon. They said they would. They wanted to come sooner, but I asked if I could, you know. Just have 5 minutes, on our own. Two us.

Talk to him.

Tell him stuff.

Just sit, for a bit.

She looks at the bed. She turns back to us. Plays with her necklace.

He give me this, when we got engaged. Couldn't afford a ring, so he give me this till we get some money.

She shows us her pendant, it is half a heart.

He's got the other half. Wears it all the time, even though, you know, they're technically for girls. Lads at work take the piss. Said he dunt care. He's funny like that.

She looks at the bed.

He dunt look too bad I think, do you think? You know considering that… He could look worse. Could look a lot worse, but… Face is a bit pale, but that's just the blood, int it? It is. The nurse told me. Cus he's lost, he has lost quite a bit I think. But that's not bad, they said. Dunt mean nothing.

Beat. She looks at the bed.

He's sleeping now.

He'll be dreaming. You can tell he is cus the way his eyes are half open. He always sleeps like that. Used to think it was weird when we first met. Like he was watching me. I don't now, think it's sort of sweet. Sort of like he's half here, and half there, half with me even in his sleep.

I bet he's having a mad one. He always has mad dreams, always waking me to tell me them going 'Lisa! Guess what!' And I'm like 'I don't care Danny it's 5 in the morning.'

Stupid. Like a kid or something.

Said he dreamt he met Obama the other night. Said it was really nice. They were having a beer in the Swan.

I tried talking to him earlier, but I couldn't think of what to say. It's not that there isn't stuff, loads of stuff I want to… but I couldn't think how to say it. Make it make sense, when it doesn't. Does it? None of this doesn't even make any…

It's not just me that's feeling it. It's everyone. Nurse keeps coming in to check on us. Ask how I'm doing. She touched my shoulder when she left the room. I think she can feel it too, this sort of, sense of devastation.

Sort of leaks out, doesn't it?

Beat. She pauses, collects herself.

They've changed his bandages, and the bag at the bottom.

That's all the blood drainin' from his chest. It's the fifth one they've changed. I've been counting. Seems like a lot dunt it?

Seems like loads, but it's not. Just normal apparently. I asked her, the nurse and she said it's dead normal 'In a procedure like this, it's to be expected', she said.

But I don't know. I think it can't be good you know? To lose that much blood, can't be good for no one.

Pause.

It's good that they left me with him, I think that was the nurse actually, I think she probably asked them. They were in two minds about letting me stay. Kept saying I'm not to touch him. I wanted to stroke his head, but they said I shouldn't. He's vulnerable to infection, apparently so they said I shouldn't really touch him – case I give him any germs. But it does feel weird. Not very natural.

Should have been here earlier. When they brought him round. They have to bring them round cus otherwise they might fall into a coma and never wake up. But it's hard you know, cus it's so big, the operation is so big. It's like the worst thing that your body can go through. It's like unimaginable almost. When you think about it.

Actually taking the heart out, it's like nothing you can even get your head round. The sort of bigness of it. It's massive. The way it changes you. The risk.

But they said they had to, said there was no choice. Said if they didn't he'd still die, just it'd be slower. Harder.

More painful.

We didn't even know there was anything wrong.

We was just going on like normal. We all was. We was happy.

Feels like my heart too.

Does that sound weird? Does that make sense? It probably sounds stupid but it does, feels like my heart too. Like it's not just him, it's me an all, like I've got a wound runnin' through me. Through my chest, this sort of hot ache where they put the knife in.

She rubs her fingers roughly down her sternum.

You should have been here earlier.

It was horrible. They said it would be, they do warn you. They said it was going to be a bit unpleasant but you don't think… You never think, anything could be…

He tried to rip it open. The wound, I think it was the pain, you know, where his heart was, it was the pain in his chest.

Had a tube down his throat so he couldn't speak, couldn't say nothing, all this stuff, this agony and he couldn't even speak, was just these noises, these like animal, sort of groans coming from him. And they was holding him down so he wouldn't move, but the look on his face, you know, like this look of like pure terror.

Like a kid.

Like a little boy.

I was with him when they put him back under, he was sort of weeping when he went off. I held his hand, stroked it, stroked the back of it. I didn't care about the germs, just wanted him to know. Know that I was with him. I think he did. I hope anyway.

They said they had to do it. Said he was making it worse for himself, wasn't really cooperating, but I'm thinking 'you've ripped open his chest and torn the heart from out his body' I don't know how it could get worse. I don't know what worse is.

They said I didn't understand, when I said that.

They said it was for the best.

That's what they keep saying. The last few weeks that's all they keep saying 'It's for the best Lisa, it'll make it right again', but we didn't even know he was sick.

I remember when they came. I was in our kitchen. They came right into my home, sat me down. This is our house. And they told me what was gonna happen. Talked me through the procedure.

Open Heart Surgery.

'It's the only possible option, so he can grow strong again, get him back to normal'

'But why him?'

'Cus he's sick, his heart, it's sick'

'But he dunt drink, dunt smoke, dunt eat shit, dunt take drugs. He's always been good. He hant done nothing wrong, why him? We're getting married next year, it dunt make sense.'

'It's for the best', that's all they say. 'It's for the best.'

She looks at the bed, turns away. She plays with her necklace.

Must only be a few minutes now. Till they try and wake him. They don't want me in here, said they thought that last time I was bad for him. They can't fuck it up this time. Cus they've only got one more chance.

'One more chance or what?' But I know, I know what they're saying. I do know

She stands up. Goes a bit closer to the bed. She puts her hand above where a man's chest would be to feel the heat coming off it. She puts it back beside her.

I look at his body and I think how lovely he is, how lovely and I can't imagine what happened to make him like this.

His lips have gone blue, his skin is cold. Looks all pale and dingy and whitewashed from everything they've done to him.

He looks tired.

They say this is the hard bit, now. That we're living in it.

But it scares me, cus it's not the tearing up that's hard. Is it, when you think about it?

It's the putting back together.

A moment. Lights down.

THINGS THAT MAKE NO SENSE

BY DENNIS KELLY

Characters

*** for three people, any age, any sex. 'Him/her' and 's/he' have been used through necessity and should not be pronounced as written (i.e. they should be spoken as either 'him' and 'he' or 'her' and 'she' depending on the sex of the character).

A, B and G, at a table, probably.

A: So we need to ask you some questions

G: Okay

A: just to ascertain some details pertaining to an incident that took place on the 14th –

G: Yeah, but it wasn't me.

   Beat.

A: Well, we just need to ascertain some detail pertaining to that

G: Okay, yeah, sure, but it wasn't me.

A: If you'd let me finish

G: Absolutely, but it wasn't –

B: Please let my colleague finish

A: Just let me finish

G: Yeah, of course, finish, but it wasn't –

A: ascertain some details in order to find out –

G: You see I wasn't in the country on the 14th.

   Beat.

B: We just need to ask you some questions

G: Okay, sorry

B: you have to stop interrupting

G: I'm just nervous

A: There's no need to be nervous

B: We just have to ask questions

A: Don't be nervous

B: but just let us ask

A: because if we don't ask we won't get anywhere

B: and then where will we be?

A: We'll be nowhere

B: Because we won't have asked the questions, will we.

A: Okay?

G: Okay.

Beat.

B: Good.

Now, where were you on the 14th?

G: I wasn't in the country

A: I'm gonna put down that you were in the country.

G: No, no, I *wasn't*, I wasn't in the country

B: Put down that s/he was in the country

G: What? No, look, I *wasn't* in the country.

B: Now, were you anywhere near Elephant and Castle?

G: No, of course I wasn't because I wasn't in the –

B: Put that down as a yes, s/he was in Elephant and castle

A: (*Writing.*) 'Yes, I was in El-e-phant…'

G: What are you doing, no, no, I wasn't anywhere near –

B: Put down that s/he was there at two fifteen

A: You were there at two fifteen?

G: No, of course I wasn't –

B: The incident took place at two fifteen

A: And you were there?

G: No!

B: Put that down as a 'yes'.

A: (*Writing.*) 'Yes, I was there…'

    G watches.

G: What are you doing? Why are you writing that? I wasn't in Elephant and Castle at two fifteen on the 14th, I was in Sweden. I was in a city called Malmo in Sweden. I was there on a business trip, I flew into Copenhagen airport and then took an intercity train, I have tickets at home, ticket stubs, my flight came in at 1.45, I took an intercity train which took about forty-five minutes, I got out of the station, I was picked up by a girl named Beate and I was taken to a hotel called the Kronstaad, I was there on business, I sell bottled water, I'm a bottled water salesperson and I was in Sweden selling bottled water.

    Pause.

B: Put down that s/he was outside Jessop's.

A: Outside Jessop's? The incident took place outside Jessop's; what were you doing outside Jessop's?

G: I wasn't there!

A: Okay, okay, I understand. But what were you doing there?

G: I wasn't doing anything because –

B: Put down buying a digital camera.

A: You were buying a digital camera?

G: No!

A: What make?

G: What are you talking about?

A: Do you have a receipt for this digital camera?

G: No, because I wasn't –

B: Could've destroyed it.

A: (*Writing.*) 'was buying a digital…'

Beat.

G: What are you doing? What is this, is this a joke? Are
       you having a joke, is this a joke, are you trying to
       rattle me? Is that what this is, you're trying to rattle
       or something? Because this is not, it's not, this is not
       funny, okay, you are not funny, you are neither of you
       funny and this is not a joke and I'm not rattled because
       I was in Sweden selling bottle water, which is my job,
       okay?

Pause. They stare at him/her.

Pause. They sit back.

B: Show him/her the photos.

Nothing.

       Go on.

*Beat. A pulls out a folder, places it on the table. Opens it. Takes
out a photo, hesitates then slides it in front of G. G looks, suddenly
recoils. They watch.*

*A takes out another, slides that across too. G is horrified by what s/
he sees. They watch.*

Another. Similar effect. They watch.

Another. Similar effect. They watch.

Pause. A gathers the photos and puts them away.

G is trying not to cry, perhaps failing.

You okay?

G nods.

Need a tissue, or…?

G shakes head.

Sure? Drink of water?

G shakes head. A sits back.

I had the same reaction. I've been doing this job for a long time. A long time. Seen a lot of things. Never seen that before. Something like that. Something like that stays with you, that will stay with you, that. It's the act of an animal, that. It's the sort of thing that makes you wonder, it's the sort of thing that makes you ask yourself what goes through a person's mind. That's the thing you can't get out of your head, that question, what goes through a person's mind, when they're doing something, something like that, something they know is doing so much… harm and wrong, what goes through their mind, how do they do it and what… just what goes through their mind?

A: That is the act of an animal.

B: Can I ask you a question?

G nods.

Do you think a crime like that should go unpunished?

Beat.

G: No, but –

B: There you are then.

G: But it wasn't me!

B: Put down 'It was me.'

A: (*Writing.*) 'It was…'

G: I said it wasn't, it wasn't, it was not, it wasn't me! I didn't do that, I did not do that, someone else did that, why should I be punished?

Pause. A shrugs.

B Shrugs.

B: Don't have a good answer for that.

A: Just the way it is.

B: it's just the way it is

A: It's wrong but there you are.

B: there you are

A: there we are

B: It's not just you. It's others as well.

A: Everywhere, this is happening, all over the country

B: Done a pensioner for GBH last night; poor old fella can hardly walk

A: Just pulled in a tramp for international money laundering, amounts in the severals of billions.

B: A little old lady for hacking into the Pentagon

A: We've got a man in a coma being questioned in connection with a series of terrorist atrocities

B: Pulled in a priest for joyriding

A: got a woman downstairs who's being done on four counts of rape

B: Yesterday I arrested a four-year-old girl as the suspected head of a Columbian drugs cartel

A: Did a teenage boy for the assassination of JFK

B: We've got an entire school lined up to go down for the Armenian genocide

A: an eight-month-old girl accused of the Great Fire of London

B: there's an unborn child in Nottingham who's facing twenty years for attempted murder

A: did a cat yesterday for piracy on the high seas

B: It's not just you

A: it's everyone

B: we're all in this together, you see

A: you're getting off lightly

B: just murder

A: just a little old murder

B: you need to see the benefits

A: you need to see the positives

B: this is a wonderful opportunity, a wonderful way to clear the books

A: all sorts of crimes are being wiped away

B: it's like year one, we're starting again

A: you need to see the positives

B: don't just think of yourself

A: you selfish shit.

G: I didn't do anything, I'm innocent!

B: Put down 'I done it, I killed him and I'm glad I killed him'

G: This is insane

B: 'I'm glad I done it and I'd do it again in a heartbeat, I'd kill him in the blink of an eye and I'd kill you too, copper, if I had the chance'

A: (*Writing.*) 'I done it, I killed…'

G: Please…

B: Sorry.

        I'm very sorry. But this is not just about you.

THE FAT MAN

BY ANDERS LUSTGARTEN

Written after a lengthy breakfast
in Exmouth Market with Simon Stephens

I went to Las Vegas once. You drive through the desert for hours, and from nowhere this shocking spectacle appears: Egyptian temples and pirate ships and pulsating neon red and yellow palm trees and white tigers in cages. A cornucopia of capitalist excess, as far as the eye can see. And then on the ground floor of the casinos, the public floor where anyone can go, the spectacle suddenly stops.

The punters on the ground floor are poor and filthy and seem to have no idea that it's Christmas Day. They're fixated on putting nickels and dimes into the slots as grimly as if they were machines keeping their loved ones alive. Now, if you want to go up to the next floor, where the atmosphere is a little less desperate, you have to cash a very specific amount of money. The floor above that, twice as much. What looks from the desert like a party to which everyone is invited turns out to be a beehive segregated by impenetrable layers of money.

Vegas is capitalism as a town. And if capitalism were a man...? Well, capitalism is not like other political systems. Fascism and communism, they're grumpy drunks at the bar: 'Come and have a go if you think you're hard enough'. Capitalism, on the other hand, is the Fat Man. The affable fat guy working the room, slapping backs, buying rounds, making everybody feel welcome. Not sloppy fat, but sleekly corpulent in the middle like a shark.

Richard. Great to see you. Have a canapé. Not for me, trying to lose a few, you know. It is a great party, isn't it? Well, we posted such robust figures, I thought we should have a little celebration. Took a few risks and they paid off, that's all.

Ladies and gentlemen: the Fat Man of Capitalism is lying to you. He lies about how he earns his money by being brave and independent and tough. Yet there's no bigger sponger off the state than the fat man. We educate his workers. We build roads for his goods. We

hire police so he can take his profits safely home. The fat man makes his money off the back of your money, always has done. And when his brave tough adventures go wrong, we bail him out. The financial crisis wasn't the point at which 'capitalism collapsed'.
It was the point when the Fat Man ate the public in the name of saving us.

How does he get away with it? A couple of ways.

In nomine Patri et Filii et Spiritu Sanctu, et Hedge Fundii derivati multi complicati, et profitum giganticum nauseatum, et crisum magnum financialis, Amen.

Like a medieval priest keeping the Bible in Latin so ordinary people don't know what's in it, the Fat Man blinds us with his patter of derivatives and credit default swaps to keep what he does opaque. Don't be afraid of the Fat Man, ladies and gentlemen. He's just a spivvy little hustler playing the shell game. You know the shell game? The object is to take the sucker's money. Watch the ball now.

(Cockney carnival barker.) *Gather round, gather round, a trillion pounds! Loans from Deutsche Bank to National Bank of Greece. Mortgage backed security from Deutsche Bank to Goldman Sachs. Collateralised Debt Obligation from Goldman Sachs to Morgan Stanley and Credit Suisse. Credit Default Swap – Failure of Greek mortgage loans. Shuffle. Shuffle.* (Beat. Renewed energy.) *Bailout! Bailout to National Bank of Greece. Bailout from National Bank of Greece to Deutsche Bank, Goldman Sachs, Credit Suisse and Morgan Stanley and which box is the ball under? Take yer time, darling. Unlucky. Better luck next time.*

This actually happened. 85% of the Greek bailout left Greece as soon as it arrived and went to the banks for loans they chose to make on the free market to the housing bubble. But the Greek government gave the banks all their money back, which means the Greek people are paying back tens of billions in bailout loans they never even saw.

Why does the Fat Man have governments over a barrel? Because when he needs to, the Fat Man gets nasty. During our bailout, our friendly neighbourhood banks threatened to turn off the ATMs if they didn't get every penny they wanted.

You see, Richard, the thing is I'm going through a period of illiquidity and I'm rather going to need the money. Really? How many? They'll find other work, I'm sure. Incentive structures. Labour market flexibility. I wouldn't want to have to take this beyond a friendly chat. "Robust figures?" Paper, Richard. On paper. Shall we say Thursday? Good man. Oh, and Richard? You never had a canapé.

So one answer is bullying, and another answer is hypnosis. "*Look into my eyes, not around the eyes, into the eyes, one two three, you're under.*" I used to study Maoism, as you do, but I've never seen a group of people as brainwashed as our governments are by Fat Man Capitalism. Brainwashed into the cuts.

There is no reason for any of the cuts. Not one. Our debt isn't unsustainable. Even after the bailout, our debt to GDP ratio is average for Western Europe. And the main thing is, there's shitloads of money out there. It's a question of who has it.

Vodafone owes £6 billion in taxes that it's not gonna pay. The UK loses £120 billion a year in tax avoidance. A 0.01% tax on City financial transactions would give us £25 billion a year. A one off 20% levy on assets over a million pounds wipes out the entire national debt.

Get the corporate welfare queens and the Monaco-domiciled, Chelsea-living, tax-dodging scum to pay us what they owe us, and the libraries and the theatres and the schools stay open. It genuinely is that simple.

And if we don't grab the Fat Man by the balls? Well, the really scary thing is, he doesn't just want your money. He wants to change the way you think. When a student leaves uni thirty grand in debt, she doesn't go to have her mind expanded and she doesn't work with animals afterwards. She sees it as a financial investment, to maximise her returns, and the Fat Man is at the controls of her brain. And is she happy? In a survey of European happiness levels, the UK came 26th out of 28. The good news is, we're ahead of Romania and Belarus.

Don't fear the Fat Man, ladies and gentlemen. Fuck the Fat Man. What happens in Vegas stays in Vegas. We don't wanna live there.

So what are we gonna do? The first thing we're gonna do is not talk ourselves out of action. (*Takes out iPhone*) I have an iPhone. Am I a hypocrite, or someone who lives in a consumer society? Does it mean I shouldn't call the Fat Man what he is? Capitalism makes us all complicit and none of us pure. Don't let that put you off.

This is politically the most exciting time to be alive in decades. For all those who think ah fuck it, things are never gonna change, this is the way things are, what about Tunisia? Egypt? Libya? Mass political change always happens suddenly and beautifully and unexpectedly. People are always the thing to trust.

Start by making yourself uncomfortable physically and morally. How much of what I have do I need? Who can I speak to about this stuff? What would a better world look like and how can we start it? Do something – go on a demo, occupy a library, poke an aristocratic parasite with a stick through the window of her car. Cause some trouble, any way you can. And keep doing it.

It starts with people, always has done. Let's get to work.

FRAGILE

BY DAVID GREIG

Characters

JACK

CAROLINE

Setting

Caroline's Office

Note on the text

The character of Caroline is intended to be spoken as a choir by the audience at the show. I think this may be best achieved by using a PowerPoint projection and putting Caroline's lines up on the screen. The audience will need to be briefed about this, and made to feel at ease with the process. I have provided a briefing here but you may use your own.

There is an art to putting up the audiences' lines. Timing is important. There is a sense in which the stage manager responsible for the PowerPoint is the other actor in the company.

Audience lines are in italics. I have indicated with a dash where I intend each slide to begin and end.

AUDIENCE BRIEFING

Hello Ladies and Gentlemen and welcome to this performance of **Fragile** by David Greig. **Fragile** is written as a dialogue between a character called Jack and a character called Caroline. But, in the spirit of austerity Britain David has asked that it should be performed by only one actor…

Obviously that leaves the other part free.

So… in the spirit of the big society David has asked if you – the audience – would be willing to step in. He asks if you would be willing to play the role of Caroline.

What's going to happen is this – (insert name here) the actor playing Jack will say his lines and then, when it is your turn to speak, a slide will come up with your lines on it. Let's try it:

(Slide)

Hello Jack.

(Audience say 'Hello Jack')

That was great let's try another.

(Slide)

We're all in this together.

(Audience say 'we're all in this together')

Brilliant!

Occasionally there will be stage directions which we would ask you to follow. Stage directions are presented in brackets. Let's try one:

(pause, look sceptical)

Excellent!

Some of you may not want to do everything on the slides. That's fine. Some of you may not want to do anything. That's also fine. For this to work we just need at least some of you to be saying each line – otherwise poor (actor's name) will be left waiting for his cue.

This is not a trick. It's meant honestly. It's intended to be enjoyable.

Feel free to act! Project! But whatever you do – don't ask:

(Slide)

What's my motivation?

(Audience might say 'what's my motivation'.)

Thank you ladies and gentlemen.

If everyone's ready – now, we'll begin.

Fragile, by David Greig.

A swivel chair,
On the swivel chair, JACK.

JACK wears a black balaclava.

At his feet sits a supermarket 'bag for life'.
Inside the bag, a flask.

JACK swigs from a bottle of lucozade sport.

JACK rehearses his introduction.

Caroline!

Caroline.

Caroline,

May I just say you look fabulous, tonight?

JACK looks about the room.

How's it hanging Caroline?

How's the drumming?
Good?
Good.

JACK spins on the chair.

Ca – ro – line

Suddenly
LX: Lights on.

Ahhhhhhhhhhh!
(*Please Scream*)

It's ok.

Get away from me!

Caroline!
Get back!
Please!
Put the lampshade down Caroline.

It's me…
Jack.
Jack.

JACK takes off the balaclava.

Oh god.
Dear god.
Jack.

Sorry.

You scared me.

It was the mask wasn't it.
I should have taken it off.
I forget the small things.
Good at the big, bad at the small.
Let's start again.
Can we start again?
Caroline?

OK Jack.
Let's start again.

Right, you go back over there,
I'll put the lights out.

LX: Lights out.

You come in.
Switch the lights on.

LX: Lights on.

Caroline!
How lovely to see you!

Hello Jack.

And may I just say, you look fabulous tonight.
Those pajama bottoms – so – and the t-shirt – very
– 'Sandanista' it says – I like old t-shirts don't you –

cuddly and soft. What is Sandanista anyway Caroline?
Is it a place?

It's difficult to explain.

Are you ok Caroline?

I'm fine, Jack.

Would you like some Lucozade Sport?

No thank you.

Are you sure?

(please look at Jack – give him a hard stare)

What?

(continue to stare hard)

What Caroline?

Jack
Are you on drugs?

I knew you'd ask me that. I knew it! Quick as a brush
– aren't you? No flies. It's like you've got eyes in every
part of your body or something. A cat!

Jack!

No – I am not on drugs.

You seem…fragile.

Do I? Yes. I expect – I can see how you would think
that, Caroline: midnight. Climbing in through your
living room window. It's an unorthodox. It's thinking
outside the box. But in fact I'm not on drugs. I'm not
fragile at all. In fact. I'm really quite robust at the
moment.

Robust.

I did have a little bit of dope.

Jesus Jack.

Sorry Caroline.

Jack,
It's 5 am.
It's extremely inappropriate for you to be in my house.
You have to go home now.
If you don't go home now I'm going to call the police.

No!
Don't do that Caroline.
Please.

Why are you here Jack?

They're going to close the centre.

Oh.

It's true isn't it?

Yes.

I found out.
Chap in a pub.
Chat chat chat.
No secrets round here

I was going to explain it all tomorrow at the group meeting.

It's all right.
Caroline.
No need to explain.

They didn't have a choice.

I know.
Primary schools.
Loonies.
Big Society.
Bang.
Our Centre
A small star in a galaxy of shiny lights.

Inevitable really.
Gone.

Mental Health Support services across the city have to find savings of 10 per cent.

I know. I know everything.

I hate this. I really do. I hate it.

Caroline I understand. Jesus. Caroline – you don't think I'd think you'd let them close the centre if you had a choice? Jesus. I know you, Caroline. You're the loveliest person I know. You're kind and you're clever and you're patient – and you stand up to people – I've seen you stand up to some actually quite big cunts and say – 'Fuck off!' – you're nice – you don't take no shit and you do that bongo drumming but you know what it's actually pretty good Caroline – you're actually surprisingly good at those bongos – we laugh at you but behind your back we actually say how much we like it –

…

What's it called the thing you do with the bongos?

Capoeira (pron Cap – ooh – erra)

That's it.
Capoeira.
Caroline – you could do anything with your time but every Tuesday and Thursday you come down to the centre with your fucking bongo drum and your fucking yoga mats and your fucking box files full of housing benefit this and forms for getting cookers that – you come down the centre and you do stuff with us and I love you for that Caroline.

Thank you Jack.

Not in a sexual way of course.

No.

Although – looking at you now in those cuddly jim jams –

If you weren't old enough to be my mother...

He winks.

(*Hard stare*)

I'm joking Caroline – it would be inappropriate for you and me to have a sexual relationship because even though you're a milf you're also my mental health support worker and I am mentally completely fucked.

Fragile.

Fragile, that's it, completely fucking fragile.

It's late, Jack.

I love going to the centre Caroline. – If something's bothering me on Saturday or Sunday or Monday – I think to myself – don't worry Jack – you'll be down at the centre on Tuesday. If it's Wednesday, I think to myself don't worry Jack – you'll soon be down at the centre tomorrow and whatever gnat's currently attacking your head – Caroline can catch it. Or Eddie. Or Mrs D.

…

Then if it's Friday I *remember* being at the centre and doing the breathing exercise or that film about the bees or your song and I feel calm – like there's a hand on my back – you know?

I know.

A hand, Caroline.

There will be support provision.
There will be an office in the new shopping centre.
It will be open on Wednesdays.

Not with you, though.

No.

They've sacked you, haven't they Caroline?

They didn't sack me.

No?

My job is freelance now.

You have the most beautiful garden Caroline. When I was trying to break in through your window just now I crawled across your lawn and do you know that my body left prints in the frost on your grass? Now that's a sight you don't see every day. You must love your garden – the birds – the bus stop over there – the road sign.

…

Do you know what Caroline?

I hate buses.

I suppose I could walk. I suppose they think I should walk. Probably I should walk to the new shopping centre on Wednesdays.

I can't walk that far.

This leg's fucked since those kids ran over my leg in the Wheatsheaf car park.

I'm sorry Jack.
It's all so complicated.

No, it's not complicated Caroline, it's simple. When someone says it's complicated what they really mean is 'it's simple but it's something I don't want to say. So I'll say it's complicated and avoid saying it.'

…

It's simple, Caroline.
We don't matter enough.

No.

It's true Caroline. If we mattered more they wouldn't
do things that are bad for us.

…

Soraya, Damon, Alisdair Macintosh, Johnny the Bang
and Itchy George, and Aisha and Welcome-In-Duane.
It's all of us, Caroline.
It's not that we don't matter at all.
We matter a bit.
It's just – we don't matter enough.

The budget to the area mental health support services has been
cut by a third.
They didn't want to salami slice.
It made more sense to make one big saving.

Caroline, have you ever heard of a person called
Mohamed Bouazizi?

No.

I didn't think you would have heard of him Caroline.

Who is Mohamed Bouazizi Jack?

Well Caroline, Mr Mohamed Bouazizi was a chap in
Tunisia and he had been generally screwed about with
and what he did – Caroline – what he did was he set
himself on fire outside the municipal offices of his town
– and what happened was when he did that – Caroline
– was that the Tunisian people got a shock – they got
a shock and they looked round their shitty Tunisian
rooms with their shitty Tunisian duvets and their shitty
Tunisian biscuits and the shit on their shitty Tunisian
kitchen floors – and they thought hang on – hang on
they thought – this is all fucked up. This situation is all
fucked up Tunisia, and we need to do something about

it. Just like I did when you came round and found
me under my wardrobe that day Caroline – I looked
around I thought this situation is all fucked up Jack and
it has to change. So now Caroline – three dictators have
gone – there's a different dictator being deposed every
day all because of Mohamed Bouazizi and what he did.
Think of that.
After you found me under the wardrobe, Caroline.
I gave up drink.
I haven't had a drink for seven months and eight days.
Things can change Caroline,
Even when you think they can't.

I can't fight anymore, Jack.
Everything I believed in, I fought for.
Everything I fought for, I was defeated.
Til there's was nothing left
but a kind of dream…
A dream of Britain.
And now
Even that's going.
I can't fight for a dream, Jack.
I will continue to try to protect mental health support services
in this council area.
That's all I can do.

Look at the tree Caroline – can you see it in the
moonlight? – can you see the way the light's glistening
on the branches? – you're going to remember that
Caroline. One Tuesday in the future you're going to be
in the centre and someone will say 'do you remember
that Monday night?' 'That Monday night Jack was in
your living room?' and you'll laugh and say, 'I do, I
remember that day very well. How could I forget it?
The frost on the tree branches, the big swivel chair, my
soft pyjamas, and that peculiar smell – And the person
will say 'What peculiar smell?' And you'll say, 'That
peculiar smell of smoke and crisps and diesel'. And the
person will say – 'Was there a nearby railway station?'

And you'll laugh and say 'No, that smell was Jack.' – 'You'll laugh and say that was the smell of Jack on the day he changed the course of fucking history – the day he lit the spark which changed the situation and made everybody look about them and say 'this duvet stinks, these biscuits have mould on them, there is shit on our kitchen floor'. You'll say, do you remember the day, the day the crowds came – first it was the centre – and then it was the library – and then it was the swimming pool, and the shops – the crowds all came and they chanted 'this situation is all fucked up and it's got to change' and they walked up to the bus station and they hijacked the buses, and they all went to London and all over the country they came in buses – marching, ten million of them Caroline, coming out from under the wardrobe, ten million people marching up to Parliament Square chanting 'this situation is all fucked up and it's got to change.'

Ten million people Caroline, imagine that.
Can you imagine that?

What have you got in your bag Jack?

A flask of diesel Caroline.
A flask of diesel from the garage up the road.

Oh Jack.

JACK opens the flask.
As he speaks JACK pours the diesel over his head and body.

Jack, you're fragile.
You need to take your lithium.

Fuck lithium Caroline.
That's what Mr and Mrs Bouazizi probably said to Mohamed.
That's what anyone would have said to Mohamed Bouazizi.
They'd have said – take your lithium Mohamed.

I would have said it – fuck sake – Caroline if I'd met
Mohammed I'd have said to him chill out Mo – take
your fucking lithium.
It's not as if you're going to fucking change anything.
But I'd have been wrong if I said that, wouldn't I
Caroline.
Because he did change, Caroline.
He changed everything.

We don't need to be so radical.
Why don't we have a sit-in?

A sit-in is interesting Caroline
But I think setting myself on fire is a better idea.
I think more people will notice if I set myself on fire.

JACK lights the lighter.

Jack!
We'll call people
We'll use the internet
We'll start a campaign.

How do I know you won't just call a taxi
And get me back on my lithium
And then next Wednesday I'll go up to the shopping
centre
To your new office
Which will be small
And you'll say blah blah blah
And I'll say blah blah blah,
And we'll forget tonight
No trees, no frost, no Lucozade Sport
And it'll be warm in your small office.
And you'll show me a letter or something.
And the old train of shittiness will just go rumbling on
down the old shitty tracks.
How do I know that won't happen Caroline?

We'll protest
I promise.

And a crowd will come
First to the centre
Then to the library
and the swimming pool
and the bus station

And London Caroline – don't forget London.

And London.

We'll go to the Houses of Parliament,

That's right.

And we'll chant.

Yes.

We're coming out from under the wardrobe.

We're coming out from under the wardrobe.

This situation is all fucked up and it has to change.

This situation is all fucked up and it has to change.

This situation is all fucked up and it has to change.

That's what we'll say.

Do you promise Caroline?

I promise.
Now, give me the lighter Jack.
Give me the lighter.
Please.

The End.

WHIFF WHAFF

BY JACK THORNE

Characters

NIGEL

JULIE

NIGEL: The problem started with –

JULIE: Problem is a presumptive word.

NIGEL: The issue was –

JULIE: The issue started with –

NIGEL: Our cat

JULIE: Lily.

NIGEL: The kids loved her –

JULIE: Sammy and Lucy. Our kids. They were right to, she was a lovely cat.

NIGEL: Lovely.

JULIE: She had this way where she'd roll over on her belly.

NIGEL: Lovely soft fur.

JULIE: Lovely soft fur.

NIGEL: She'd mew with happiness whenever you'd walk into a room.

JULIE attempts to make the cat noise.

NIGEL smiles and attempts to make the noise too.

JULIE gets it a bit better.

NIGEL: Slightly lower.

JULIE adjusts her tone.

NIGEL: She's better at that sort of stuff than me.

JULIE: I've always been good with voices.

NIGEL: Do your Boris Johnson.

JULIE: No.

NIGEL: She does an amazing Boris. She even does the arm movements. It's very funny. She does this thing where she turns the thing he said about whiff whaff into whiff whaff paddywhack give a dog a bone. It's very funny. And don't get her started on the bikes.

JULIE: We first noticed a problem when Lily started moving more gingerly.

NIGEL: Well, not gingerly so much as differently – she had a very altered gait.

JULIE: She was putting her weight on all parts of her except her left leg.

NIGEL: She started having trouble getting up after she lay down.

JULIE: She couldn't get up the stairs.

NIGEL: We took her to the vets: Osteoarthritis.

JULIE: She had cats arthritis. Or degenerative joint condition. He gave us some medication. But he told us it was degenerative.

NIGEL: I don't like that word degenerative.

JULIE: Our Lily was never going to get better.

NIGEL: Now – we – me and Julie – are not the sort of person to lie down and accept such a condition.

JULIE: Because you can do that? Can't you? You can accept, or you can reject, you can challenge or you can die.

NIGEL: It was small and subtle the changes we made at first. Changes to help her in getting over her problems –

JULIE: Issues.

NIGEL: Issues.

JULIE: Putting her food at the top of the stairs.

NIGEL: Took most of the morning sometimes for her to get up those stairs. And she'd rarely be able to get down again, one time –

JULIE: This is brilliant –

NIGEL: One time I saw her look at the stairs down – much harder on the joints when you're descending – I saw her look at the stairs – sigh – and then literally make the decision to drop off the top of the first floor landing to the floor below. She didn't land on her four legs. Her left leg was buggered, of course she didn't. And she made quite a racket on landing. It hurt her. But she was down. I admired that.

JULIE: Lot to admire in that.

NIGEL: The next stage – the next thing we did was to tie very small weights to her hind legs, just to encourage her to think of all her legs as disabled. She made quite a fuss about that too.

JULIE: And we had several more stages in mind. Including wiring her jaw. But she died. So we never got to try them out.

NIGEL: We buried her in the garden. Said a few words.

JULIE: It was quite moving.

Pause.

NIGEL: When Sammy was hit by the train we were initially very upset.

JULIE: Very upset. It was quite a shock. He had his legs amputated from the knee down.

NIGEL: But then we realised we needed to think of it as an opportunity. An opportunity to prove that he didn't need support to function in society.

JULIE: He had troubles yes. Issues.

NIGEL: He had trouble sitting on seats, he had trouble lying in bed. So initially he was allowed –

JULIE: Permitted.

NIGEL: To use a belt to support himself. But after a month – we took it away – we'd made clear to him that it was a temporary support allowance. So he lay on the floor after that. And slept on the floor.

JULIE: Getting rid of the wheelchair shocked – everyone.

NIGEL: But as we said – what is mobility if it's aided. That's not real mobility. Real mobility is...

JULIE: Real mobility is being mobile without support.

NIGEL: We discussed crutches – but crutches – well, as the name implies, they're a crutch.

JULIE: Yes. He had to crawl – well, drag – himself – along the street.

NIGEL: But boy did he get some admiring glances.

JULIE: He was on board with it. All the way. We didn't even need to ask him.

NIGEL: Do your Boris voice...

JULIE: No.

NIGEL: When the lesions in his arms grew septic. It shocked everyone. But it wasn't a problem –

JULIE: Issue –

NIGEL: He could still pull himself along on his stumps. And so that's what he did.

JULIE: No one saw the car coming.

NIGEL: There were those who said he had to work jolly hard to make sure his head was exactly beneath the wheel that killed him. But we said – well, then if that's true, if he did do that work, then good on him.

JULIE: But we prefer to think of it as an accident.

Pause.

NIGEL: When I developed early on-set Alzheimer's – initially we were stumped...

JULIE: I won't say it was a problem but it was certainly an issue –

NIGEL: Because I didn't...

JULIE: We refused all medication of course. And then we put our heads together and asked: what would David do.

NIGEL: There are mornings when I can't remember Julie, can't remember – can't remember – my daughter – s – name.

JULIE: But he comes through it.

NIGEL: What's her name?

JULIE: I confess there are times when I get worried.

NIGEL: What's our daughter's name?

JULIE: One time – he didn't come home for three days – he'd gone to get some milk and been taken by an – urge – they said – the police said – why didn't he have any identification in his wallet – I said because identification encourages weakness.

NIGEL: What's her name? Is it Laura...Laura...

JULIE: He's been brought back four or five times now. The neighbours stare at us funny. But the neighbours have stared funny at us for years. They don't understand our ways.

NIGEL: Laura...Lily...no, that's our cat... Some things I remember really well...

JULIE: (*Boris impression.*)

Whiff Whaff Paddlewhaff Give A Dog A Bone.

This old lag came rolling home.

A ha!

I did.

A ha.

Pause.

JULIE: It isn't as good as he thinks it is.

NIGEL: Lucy.

HOUSEKEEPING

BY LUCY KIRKWOOD

Characters

COAL

JOAN

MRS DEAN

COAL and JOAN. JOAN is a woman old enough to be a mother. COAL might be a man or a woman, and in fact may appear to be both at times. COAL's name is not only one cheap pun but two.

A long pause.

COAL: Have you considered the sea.

JOAN: The sea.

COAL: Don't dismiss it. It might be a thought.

JOAN: Yes but we swim. Every morning.

COAL: Not all of you.

JOAN: The others watch from the beach. We take our swimming goggles and our swimming hats wrapped up in a towel like a sausage roll and we run down the shingle and into the water. Even in winter, even in February. It makes you gasp at first but the pleasure.

COAL: How much

JOAN: What?

COAL: The enjoyment the, I'm sorry, the pleasure. That you get from this, um, activity, could you place it on some sort of scale for me?

JOAN: Quantify the light on the water and the blood rushing to your skin?

COAL: No don't.

JOAN: I'm sorry what did I, what?

COAL: I can't get into that sort of emotive language.

JOAN: What you're saying is making me emotive, because I know what you're implying what you're thinking / and it's, it's making me a bit sick actually literally actually –

COAL: Joan. Joan. Joan! Joan Joan listen to me I'm not asking you to sell it.

,

JOAN: You're not – I thought –

COAL: You jumped ahead.

JOAN: When you said consider the sea –

COAL: You jumped the gun.

JOAN: You didn't mean / as a –

COAL: Come on.

JOAN laughs.

JOAN: I am so sorry, / this is –

COAL: Don't be. Crossed wires!

JOAN: Getting carried away again

COAL: That's so you.

JOAN: You're right, it is, that's so me.

COAL: Getting carried away again.

JOAN: I've always been like it.

COAL: I know you have! It's the reason why we love you.

JOAN: Only. My insides went like a bag of snakes, you saying things like that.

COAL: Part of the reason.

JOAN: I was getting ready to thump you one! In my head I was like: if they're suggesting that I sell off the sea, then that is not on and I won't stand for it!

COAL: When all I'm talking about is a small *fraction* of the total liquid.

,

JOAN: A fraction.

COAL: A fraction.

JOAN: I'm sorry.

COAL: Fifteen percent say.

JOAN: No.

COAL: No but no don't, you, because this is academic isn't it, until an actual sum has been proposed.

He takes out a piece of paper, writes a number on it and shows her.

JOAN: Is that a zero?

COAL: That's five zeroes, that I've expressed interpretively through one very large zero.

JOAN: Why is the zero wearing a top hat?

COAL: Why not?

,

JOAN: Well. Fifteen. Perhaps if was just fifteen.

COAL: Exactly.

JOAN: I mean fifteen is quite...

COAL: Negligible, exactly. Because fifteen percent, that's quite a small amount, isn't it? I suspect you would barely notice its absence.

JOAN: Fifteen percent

COAL: Or twenty.

JOAN: Twenty.

COAL: Nice round number twenty.

JOAN: Fifteen's a round number.

COAL: Twenty's rounder. More round.

JOAN: Is this really necessary?

COAL: Where is that question coming from and please don't tell me because I think I can guess.

,

JOAN: There was a woman

COAL: That woman.

JOAN: You know who I'm talking about?

COAL: I know exactly the type of woman you're talking about, you didn't let her in I hope?

JOAN: Yes but

COAL: Jesus Christ.

JOAN: She knocked at the door.

COAL: Clever. That's exactly what I'd expect from that type of woman.

JOAN: She had a trouser suit on.

COAL: Of course she did – that type of woman – you know what I'm about to say, don't you?

JOAN: Of course but

COAL: That type of woman believes in homeopathy.

JOAN: No. / I don't think so.

COAL: Yes. Yes that type of woman believes in a plethora of hare-brained things that include, but are not limited, to homeopathy.

JOAN: She was pleasant enough.

COAL: That type of woman demands OBEs for hippies, she wants to make roads from wheat, she wants to subsidize gypsies, she wants all new-born children to be fitted with solar panels, she believes in the recycling of dreams and that foxes are entitled to disability benefits she is the face of National Quorn Day. She has campaigned / long and hard

JOAN: I read her pamphlet.

COAL: Long and / hard.

JOAN: It didn't mention any of this.

COAL: Long and hard for the enfranchisement of fungi.

JOAN: She didn't mention –

COAL: She wants to give mushrooms the vote.

JOAN: She brought me a plant.

COAL: Well. Plants. I might have brought you a plant. A gifted plant is a Trojan horse I'm surprised you couldn't see through that.

JOAN: I'm sorry.

COAL: It's okay.

Joan? Joan?

It's okay.

JOAN: Yes. Only she said –

COAL: Here we go. Here we eff word go. I hope you told her. In the last ten months you have ceased all purchases of tea-bags, soap, bread and toilet paper, light-bulbs, newspapers, electricity, toothpaste, water, milk, contraceptives, wheelchairs and stethoscopes and why would all that be necessary, why would I as your accountant demand such stringent measures – and I do recognize them to be stringent – if it weren't for that fact that – I can't even say his name it makes me that angry –

JOAN: Leonard.

COAL: – if it weren't for the fact that Leonard, thank you (who is the only accountant I know who owns and regularly uses a Fisher Price calculator) had left you in such a complete and total bloody pickle?

JOAN: Yes, I told her all that. And she got this funny look on her face and she said she couldn't help noticing you'd started construction on the mono-rail in the back garden.

And she said in fact, if you look at other families like us, sort of, elsewhere, we were actually…alright. / Maybe.

COAL: She doesn't understand the numbers.

JOAN: She said she could come back and explain the numbers to me if I wanted.

COAL: The numbers are very complicated. The numbers are so complicated that we need an entirely new language or something of that sort to express them.

JOAN: A new language.

COAL: Or something of that sort.

You see, I am not just your accountant Joan. I am your translator. And your friend. But if you aren't happy (because I'm sensing some hostility) perhaps I should just ring Leonard up and tell him you've changed your mind and want him back.

Would you like Leonard back, Joan? Leonard, feeling down the back of your sofa for loose change when you're not looking? Creeping round your garden at night to do his business in your nasturtiums? Walking around your nice house with his face like a fart in a jar? Is that what you want Joan?

JOAN: No.

COAL: No. I'm putting down twenty percent of the sea. Is that okay Joan?

He looks at JOAN. JOAN does not contest this.

Okay. That's banked. That's safe. We got there! It was tough, wasn't it Joan, but together we got there! You know I think I understand, for the very first time in my life, the meaning of the phrase 'Blitz spirit'.

What next?

JOAN: Isn't that enough?

An elderly woman enters.

COAL: Oh no. No we've only just started good evening Mrs
Dean.

She looks at him. She sits down.

That's it, sit down, sit down.

JOAN: Put your feet up darlin. You want a Bovril?

COAL stares at MRS DEAN who pays him no heed.

(*To COAL.*) Alright. What about. What about if you took
some of the paintings. And the instruments. And the
theatre, you can take that, it's only gathering dust.

COAL: Joan. Please.

JOAN: What?

COAL: I'm having a thought. I wonder, would you mind?

JOAN: What?

COAL: Just a little blue sky you know

JOAN: Thinking.

COAL: That's it, let's have a look at the teeth.

*He approaches MRS DEAN, she bats him away but he persists. He
squeezes her jaw to open her mouth and examines her teeth.*

COAL: Lovely. All present and correct. No wooden choppers
for you eh Mrs Dean?

MRS DEAN: Get away.

JOAN: It's alright. She's here to help.

COAL: No arthritis here! Lovely lubricated hinges.

She swings her arm from side to side, MRS DEAN pushes him off.

MRS DEAN: Cold hands.

COAL: Warm heart!

JOAN: Good pastry.

They all laugh.

COAL: No incontinence to speak of, is there? Don't mind me
Mrs Dean, just pop your bottom up for a…

He eases her up and feels her bottom.

Dry as a bone!

JOAN: Alright that's enough now.

COAL: I think. I might be speaking too hastily. But. I really
think this might clear a substantial portion of the debt.

JOAN: This? You mean.

COAL: A substantial portion.

,

JOAN: She's my grandmother.

*COAL takes out a piece of paper and writes a number on it. He gives
it to JOAN. He looks at it then passes it back. He looks at MRS DEAN.*

What would happen –

COAL: Oh I wouldn't like to.

JOAN: I would need to know.

COAL: She would be –

He looks at MRS DEAN. Whispers.

S-O-L-D. Obviously.

MRS DEAN: I can spell.

JOAN: Alright Gran. To who?

COAL: To whom.

JOAN: To whom?

    ,

COAL: If you're asking me is there a possibility that your grandmother may be built on, then yes Joan, there is that possibility. That possibility is there. I wouldn't like to lie to you and claim that it wasn't. But –

JOAN: It's out of the question.

COAL: But –

JOAN: It's out of the question.

COAL: **NOT EVERYTHING CAN BE OUT OF THE QUESTION JOAN SOMETHING HAS TO BE IN THE QUESTION.**

You live in a burning house and when your house is burning you don't run in and out rescuing every last beloved possession, you pick something as you flee through the flaming rafters, you pick something, one thing, maybe two, and later on, when the insurance claims are filed and the ruins are smoking, you are just grateful to have that meaningful photograph or that irreplaceable china figurine, and you are especially grateful to the firefighters who put out the blaze, it is possible that you bake them a cake to show your appreciation, or have your children make moving home-made cards with glitter pens, you certainly do not go round to the fire-station and start giving them shit because they were unable to salvage your pepper grinder.

    ,

JOAN: You'll find her wash-bag in the downstairs toilet. She can't digest shellfish.

JOAN exits.

MRS DEAN: What's happening? Why have you upset my Joany?

COAL: Joany isn't upset. Joany is relieved.

MRS DEAN: All night she stays up, worrying about the money. That's you, making her fret. Show me the sums, I'll bet you a liquorice dib dab this is mountains out of molehills.

COAL: You wouldn't understand the numbers.

MRS DEAN: I've got a head for numbers. Both my husbands said as much.

COAL: The numbers would be impenetrable to you.

MRS DEAN: I kept the books during a war for the Ministry of Defence.

COAL: Lovely stories.

MRS DEAN looks at COAL.

MRS DEAN: I've seen you before only your handbag was smaller and you had a string of pearls round your neck and I often thought about what it would feel like to rip them off and show your white grasping throat to the world. Has anyone old ever told you what it was like when they were a girl?

COAL: Where's this wash-bag then?

COAL exits.

MRS DEAN: I met a man in Epping Forest, hundreds of years ago this was, and he said to me they're buying up the land, they're fencing off the trees, they won't let me gather my wood here any more and I said well that won't do so we went to see the Queen and she put a stop to it. This was back in the day when she had the nice red hair and the heart of a king, not a pack of rats on strings and no power except to throw off the timings of my Christmas Dinner.

COAL returns with MRS DEAN's wash-bag.

COAL: Stinks of face powder and smelling salts. Do you own such a thing as a spare pair of knickers?

MRS DEAN: I walked through Jarrow and I kept walking back and back until I got to Putney in time to see old big nosed Ollie Cromwell take his seat. Colonel Rainsborough was in a flap and couldn't get his words in order so I told him what to say and what he said was 'I think that the poorest he that is in England hath a life to live as the greatest he' and later that day when the Beveridge report came out I danced through the bombsites of Coventry shouting EN AITCH ES! EN AITCH ES! and I let a policeman kiss me I was crying I was that happy.

COAL: Lovely stories.

MRS DEAN: How much will you get for me?

COAL: I'm confident we'll achieve the asking price.

MRS DEAN: How much is that?

COAL: You're doing your bit.

MRS DEAN: You said I'd be built on.

COAL: That's only one scenario. If you're lucky you may be purchased by the local community.

MRS DEAN: They might not have enough money. You told them they were skint

COAL: They could have a fete. A charity raffle. A sponsored growth of facial hair. The fundraising possibilities are infinite.

MRS DEAN: But if they don't.

COAL: It's up to your friends and neighbours to assume responsibility for you. If they choose not to then that is unfortunate, and reflects badly upon their character.

MRS DEAN: What will I become?

COAL: A power station that heats the home of an elderly couple during a cold winter. A new house in which a desperate family are re-homed. A Centre Parcs where child carers get some much needed 'me-time'.

MRS DEAN: I don't know what that is.

COAL: Me-time?

MRS DEAN: Centre Parcs

COAL: Water slides. Designated bridleways for plump Shetland ponies. Wooden chalets. Karaoke in the evenings and breakfast buffets.

MRS DEAN begins to cry.

MRS DEAN: I don't like karaoke.

COAL: Public isn't always good.

MRS DEAN: I'd like to have a swim / before we go.

COAL: Public isn't always economically viable the car is waiting.

MRS DEAN: I've swum in that sea every day since I was five years old. Swallowed all sorts I expect. Hundreds of years of other people's urine and skin cells and dandruff and germs and whatnots. It's like a soup that sea, a leveling soup, a minestrone where the peas are as good as the pasta. I'm fetching me bathers.

COAL: Which part of the sea did you want to, ah, swim in exactly?

MRS DEAN: Well. The bit near the beach I should imagine.

COAL: That particular part of the sea has recently been purchased. It's private property, unless you were to go through the proper channels, obtain bathing rights and so forth, you'd technically be breaking the law.

MRS DEAN: I'll swim in the other bit then.

COAL: The other bit.

MRS DEAN: The bit past the bit what's been sold.

COAL: Yes but you'd have to swim through the bit near the beach to get to that, wouldn't you?

MRS DEAN: I could swim under it. I can hold my breath for a full minute.

COAL laughs.

MRS DEAN: Don't laugh at me.

When no one's about I take off my clothes and I go in wearing my birthday suit and I let the salt get to all of me and afterwards I lie on a thin lilac towel and smoke a cigarette and let the sun dry me push my fingers through the pebbles and I think this is one good thing that I can touch every day and that anyone can touch it and that's good and that's magic it's like a warm dry bed or a drip that anyone can have stuck in their arm to make them better or books to read when you can't afford candles or –

COAL: Lovely stories.

COAL drags her across the floor. She wriggles from COAL's grasp.

MRS DEAN: I recognize you now. I had a dream twenty years ago I crept into your bedroom and I slit your wrists.

COAL: Lovely.

MRS DEAN: You're a cunt.

I never used that word before. It's clear to me now I was saving it up for this moment.

Blackout.

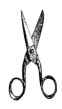

A BIGGER BANNER

BY MARK RAVENHILL

Characters

SHONA

RAQUEL

MARGE

FRED

2011. Large room in a university administration building.

RAQUEL: What do you mean? Had enough?

SHONA: Had enough of all this. The occupation.

RAQUEL: So what do you want to do?

SHONA: I've had enough of meetings all day long. Had
      enough of no clean clothes, no proper place to wash.
      Had enough of marmite sandwiches. Had enough
      sleeping on the floor.

RAQUEL: I keep you warm don't I?

SHONA: Yeah course.

RAQUEL: Cuddled up tight in the sleeping bag.

SHONA: Smelly. Three weeks – it's a smelly sleeping bag.

RAQUEL: We're all smelly. No one notices anymore.

SHONA: The first demo – so exciting. Yeah really felt powerful.

RAQUEL: We were. We are.

SHONA: Being kettled – made me so angry. I wanted to take
      them all on.

RAQUEL: I love your anger.

SHONA: But now … What we going to do? We're a group of
      kids aren't we?

RAQUEL: No. No.

SHONA: They're going to go ahead with their cuts and their
      fees and do whatever they want to do. Nothing we can
      do to –

RAQUEL: Hey listen. Listen to me. We all get tired. Get a bit
      down. I get like that few times a day. But I'm here

because … because of all the big stuff yeah but also because of you. Because I love you.

SHONA: And I love you.

RAQUEL: And I love you angry and – yeah – a bit smelly.

SHONA: Perve.

RAQUEL: Takes one.

They go to kiss. The lights go off.

SHONA: Bastards. They've done it. University said they were going to do it and now they've done it.

RAQUEL: No internet. No heat. No light. Bastards. Here. I'm prepared. No surrender.

(*RAQUEL gets a couple of nightlights from her backpack and lights them.*)

SHONA: How long are we going to keep this up?

RAQUEL: As long as it takes.

SHONA: This has got to end. Sometime.

RAQUEL: When we've won.

SHONA: We're not going to stay here forever.

RAQUEL: Don't think about it. Just get through the day. Think of the bigger picture. We need a banner for tomorrow. You make a start on that. I'm gonna get these [nightlights] to the others.

SHONA: Yeah okay.

RAQUEL: Back soon.

SHONA: Yeah.

(*They kiss. Exit RAQUEL. SHONA starts to make a banner. Stops.*)

SHONA: Oh. What's the point? Students playing games. Who's going to listen to that?

FRED and MARGE off:

FRED: But gradualism will never be effective in –

MARGE: This is not the Soviet Union. Conditions here are completely –

FRED: There are many different models for a revolutionary –

MARGE: And there are many different models for …

SHONA: Hello? Who's that? You part of the occupation?

Enter FRED and MARGE. Both are dressed in the fashions of 1950.

SHONA: Fancy dress.

MARGE: You got a smoke?

FRED: Clean out.

MARGE: Damn. I could really do with a smoke.

FRED: Me too.

MARGE: Mint's the next best thing. (*Offers.*) Want one?

FRED: Why not?

SHONA: How did you get in here? We're locked in. They're locked out. So how did you…?

FRED: If you succumb to gradualism –

MARGE: If you fantasise about revolution.

SHONA: I'm Shona. I'm one of the original occupiers. Who are you? Welcome.

SHONA holds out her hand. Pause.

MARGE: Did you hear something?

FRED: No.

MARGE: Listen. I'm sure there's a noise.

SHONA: Look are you Young Tories? Sorry. But your clothes
are kind of – odd.

MARGE: Can you hear it? Distant noise.

FRED: Rain on the roof.

MARGE: I suppose. Rain on the roof.

SHONA: So can you…? Can you not see me or hear me? Why
can't you see me or hear me?

FRED: My mouth feels fresh. Good mint.

MARGE: Yes. Mouth's very fresh.

FRED and MARGE kiss passionately.

SHONA: Ok. So I guess you can't see me. How long are you
going to be doing that? Because I've got a banner to
make.

MARGE: Do you have any protection?

FRED: No. I'm clean out. What shall we do?

SHONA: Oh god.

MARGE moves to FRED but then pulls away.

MARGE: Better not.

FRED: Yes. Absolutely. Better not.

SHONA: You're from another time. What time are you from?
I'm guessing 1948? 1950? 52? But why are you here?

FRED: Gradualism will never work. You think any gradualist
government is ever going to get rid of the hydrogen
bomb?

MARGE: I think –

FRED: No of course not. You sit around in meetings and committees waiting for Britain gradually to turn into a socialist state – and we'll all be blown sky high by the hydrogen bomb before –

MARGE: The Soviets have a hydrogen bomb so I hardly –

FRED: They do now but only because of the aggressive acts of the Allies in –

MARGE: So I don't think revolution is the only answer to –

FRED: What are you scared of? What's so frightening?

MARGE: I'm not scared I'm –

FRED: Yes there will be blood there will be terror. We will fight on the streets. But that is how the working class takes control of the state. If you think there's any other way that the capitalists will let us take control –

MARGE: Why are you such a pessimist?

FRED: I hardly think the working class fighting to own the means of production is a pessimistic attitude.

MARGE: Yes because you don't trust people. You don't trust their instinct for fairness. You think only if you hold a gun to their head will anyone change.

FRED: I don't think the capitalists are going to walk away from the banks and the factories and just hand over the keys.

MARGE: The fight you're fighting – it's the old fight. The Twenties, the Thirties but now –

FRED: Now there's a bomb to blow up the world.

MARGE: This is a different world. We own the country now. The people.

FRED: We hardly own a damn thing.

MARGE: It's begun. We're starting to own it. It can't be rolled back. It will go on and on. The coal, the railways, the shipyards. Ours. It's our health service, our schools, our social housing. Gains because of the democratic will of the –

FRED: Because the machinery of war allowed it to –

MARGE: Because we defeated fascism and now we're using that machinery to create our world.

FRED: Too slowly.

MARGE: Slowly but –

FRED: How long do you give it?

MARGE: Thirty, forty –

FRED: We'll be old and grey or dead –

MARGE: Sixty years tops.

FRED: 2010?

MARGE: By the year two thousand and ten, after we've slowly, slowly argued our case, worked on the committees, put the laws in place … yes, very dull stuff, no boys fighting on the streets, sorry – but in sixty years we'll have got there. Done it. Housing, health, jobs, education for all. A democracy of equal citizens sharing equally the wealth of the country.

FRED: I'll be eighty-one.

MARGE: Good housing, good pension –

FRED: You'll be eighty. Don't you want it now?

MARGE: This is for them. The future. Imagine a woman like me but in the future, woman from an ordinary background. I can see her.

SHONA: See me? Really?

FRED: I can't.

MARGE: I can.

SHONA: Looking straight at me. But you don't ... you can't see me.

MARGE: She takes it for granted. Stable economy, properly managed – full employment. Decent social housing. Local school shared by people of every background. Excellent health service used by all. And if she wants to go to university – well, then, society sees what an excellent thing that is for the future of the country and society pays for her to go there.

SHONA: Nice idea.

FRED: Nice idea.

SHONA: And maybe it almost happened once –

FRED: But if you think we're going to get it without a fight. It will be a fight. Fight to get it. Fight to defend it. There will have to be a revolution.

SHONA: I'm so sorry – It didn't happen. Maybe sometime, I don't know, Nineteen-Fifties or Sixties, started to get there but now – It's all going away now. All of that – being taken away.

MARGE: You really think history can be rolled back? You really think people are going to vote for anything other than an equal share of the wealth? You really think that any government could get voted in who was going to take away jobs, housing, education from the people?

FRED: I think the capitalists will fight dirty and we have to –

MARGE: Fight fight fight. Stuck in the past. The war's over. Now it's the slow work. Now it's democracy. Now it's the work to make that woman's life the best that any human being can have.

FRED: Naïve.

MARGE: Practical.

FRED: Dreamer.

MARGE: Revolution is the ultimate fantasy, dream of the –

FRED: Strange how unattractive dreaming can make a girl.

MARGE: Strange how childish talk of revolution makes a man.

FRED: There's jazz in the –

MARGE: No.

FRED: Come along for a –

MARGE: No. Thank you.

FRED: Oh. Very well. Good night.

Exit FRED.

SHONA: Can you really see me?

MARGE: Oh.

SHONA: You can.

MARGE: You're the girl from the future.

SHONA: Yes I am the girl from the future.

MARGE: Your clothes are rather … different.

SHONA: I normally scrub up better than this. Been in this for three weeks, sleeping on the floor so –

MARGE: I didn't think you'd actually appear. Made you up. Win my argument with Fred. Communists are terrible bullies aren't they?

SHONA: I was in the SWP my first term.

MARGE: SWP?

SHONA: It's a political – Socialist Workers.

MARGE: I was right wasn't I?

SHONA: Now I'm part of a broader group who oppose the –

MARGE: That's why you're here, yes? Because – more or less – I'm right. Really, it can't be any other way. The future is a more decent, equal place isn't it?

SHONA: Listen –

MARGE: And you – you have social housing, national health, jobs, you live in a more equal society.

SHONA: We have –

MARGE: And now – you have a place at university? Yes?

SHONA: Yes. I'm at university.

MARGE: So – it worked – democracy delivered a better world. Yes?

SHONA: It …

MARGE: Ghost of the future. Tell me. The truth.

SHONA: It. (*Long pause.*) Yes. Everything. Just as you said it.

MARGE: Oh yes. I knew. I'm going to tell Fred. I'm right. Put a stop to all his silly revolution talk.

SHONA: No. No. Let him. If that's his thing. If that's what keeps him fighting then revolution talk is fine.

MARGE: But if I've won the –

SHONA: No. What I told you … it's … Our secret, okay?

MARGE: I don't see why we have to –

SHONA: Ghost of the future. Our secret.

MARGE: Alright then. If you like. Strange girl.

Exit MARGE.

SHONA: Lied to her. Lied to her.

SHONA yells in rage and tears up her banner. Then SHONA crumples in tears. Enter RAQUEL.

RAQUEL: Hey come on, come on. It's alright. Stress. Tired. Alright.

SHONA: Why did I lie to her?

RAQUEL: Tore up the banner.

SHONA: Yeah.

RAQUEL: Why did you do that?

SHONA: It's not enough.

RAQUEL: Listen – if this is doing your head in then … we'll stop. Have a break. No point if it's stressing you out.

SHONA: It's not that it's …

RAQUEL: Home and in your own bed. Alright?

SHONA: No. I wanna carry on.

RAQUEL: You don't have to.

SHONA: And this [banner]. I'm going to start again. Much bigger.

RAQUEL: No more candles left.

SHONA: Don't care. Right then. Great big banner. Better get to work.

RAQUEL: You angry?

SHONA: Totally angry.

RAQUEL: I love you angry.

SHONA: Best feeling in the world.

End.

HI VIS

BY CLARA BRENNAN

Characters

LINDA/the GLOW CLOWN

Place

A residential care home for neurological
rehabilitation – outside the communal day room.

Time

A Friday in the near future

LINDA/the GLOW CLOWN enters, in full clown make-up, with clown attire – from the waist up. Below she wears a pair of jeans. A hi-vis fluorescent workman's tabard is tucked into her back pocket. She holds a handbag – inside this is a wig, hair net and red nose. She puts this down.

LINDA/the GLOW CLOWN: On my way here I frequent sex shops and women's emporiums and buy the latest pleasure gadgets. I've bought my daughter a new g-spot stimulator. It's a nifty little red one, rubbery, with a snub nose, and it's called the *Corsa. (She reaches into the bag for the hair net.)* That made my husband laugh. "What'd you go for" he says, "a 1.3 diesel or a 1.4 litre petrol?!" Yes, yes, so I inadvertently bought the super-mini of the vibrator world. Ahh, he does have a habit of extending your jokes in lieu of his own does my husband, cos he then said "As they says on *Top Gear* 'the ride is firm but well-controlled, noise is generally more abated and the driving position is fine, if slightly tall – you sit *on* a Corsa rather than in it." *(She rolls her eyes.)* Ha bloody Ha. Still, at least it's quiet and she can get a firm grip on it. Because a woman's orgasm has never been so political. *(She puts on the hair net, tucking her hair into it.)* You see my daughter has – a secret. She's in possession of a miracle.

People think we stopped at the one child because we didn't want to risk the same thing happening again. But that couldn't be further from the truth! But then of course if you do go on and have another child, one or two more, and they're healthy or mentally 'able', people think you kept trying to – compensate. As if you had had all boys and kept going til you got a girl! *(Brightly.)* No – we looked at her, and we thought that's it, she's perfect! I don't give a hoot what other people assume these days. You become quite brazen when your daughter's doubly incontinent!

I don't mind saying to the pitiers "What would you rather, you daft sod? That at birth someone had seen the signs immediately and said 'Linda – would you like us to take your daughter by the ankles and swing her little head against the wall? Tell your husband she died in the birth canal?"' Better off dead. That's what flashes across people's faces, it's "would she have been 'better-off-dead'?" My daughter?

So. About this miracle. A team of scientists from Italy are planning to come over to visit us to assess things, Doctor Salvatore – bit of a 'silver fox', fifty-two, works out, handmade shirts – wants to fly his whole team over. And do they all look like you, Doctor Salvatore, I wonder? His team, these pediatric neurologists, have built little humanoid robots in Rome. That encourage our children to walk. It's about mirror neurons these days you see. (*Poor Italian accent.*) "Is a missing link – between a-A and-a-B!" they say. It's not in the muscles! It's in the *brain,* before we're even *talking* about the muscles! Cos back in the day we had a specialist saying it's her *limbs,* this condition is in the *muscles,* that's why she can't control – So anyway, moving with the times Linda! They're ever-so cute the little things, like that Wall-E, not threatening in the least. They've got some robots that have a handle and the kids learn to handshake, and the robot nudges them gently if the child's hand goes off course, and then these ones for the lower body where little robots moonwalk backwards, mimicking the actions of the children's parents – cos if you walk backwards away from them they can mirror you and walk forwards! Through those mirror neurons, it's how we grasp another person's experiences, it's how we empathise, how we understand *another* person's pain even when *we* don't feel it. My god, it's early days but the amount of neuroscience I get through on the toilet! Thank heavens for the modern age. A hundred years ago we would have been told to lock her up and walk away and never hope. And she'd be in an asylum I don't doubt. Or a tiny overgrown mossy graveyard on the asylum's grounds: no bigger, no more resplendent, than an old pet cemetery. Anyway, to the miracle: at first I had my doubts about the Italians: "What, you want to come and assess my daughter. A virgin, in possession of a miracle? Oh you lot would love that!" But, as it turns out, not all Catholics are creepy.

So – when she turned fourteen – she ballooned a little, little bit of puppy fat, she went from being like 'two aspirins on an ironing board' to having a *great* big pair of knockers from my side! – we couldn't look after her any more. Not 24/7. I fell over with her one day when I was hefting her out the bath and I slipped a disc and she cracked her head on the basin and down we both went, her naked and soaking wet and me beneath her. (*She reaches into the bag for the wig.*) And I couldn't move, and she couldn't get up, and we lay like that, both of us in agony, pinned to each other for hours, until my husband came home and found us. But do you know, even lying there with her crushing me, we'd both managed to fall sound asleep! (*She puts on the wig.*) And after a few more slips and falls, including the one before the electric wheelchair which I can't bear to talk about, and with her needing so much physio and occupational therapy, and winching in and out of bed and her wheelchair, and three people to lift her 'safely', and my husband having to work, and her being fed through a tube – here's the phrase: We had to 'put' her in a home. And that's when it really hit me – I'm already out-living her.

Doctor Salvatore Bellini. Like the cocktail. "Is very common name" he says.

There's mild flirting on the phone since his English's so good, and – it takes a certain mind to be funny in another language, it took us a while to translate my phrase 'flicking the bean'. I said "for god's sake Salvatore don't write that in your laboratory memos!" But I've told him that he can't expect a warm reception from my daughter. I've explained to him about us killing ourselves off. How we've orphaned her. He's a good listener, and I don't mind saying I've had a few erotic dreams about him in white jeans on a Vespa.

He's said the husband and I should go out and visit his hometown on the Amalfi coast. His family used to have a floating restaurant that was moored to a jetty, and he said when he was young he used to have a toy harpoon. "Whatever for?" I asked him. And it took a long while, but he explained that he harpooned Medusas. (*Italian.*) Si, Medusa. (*Her.*) Medusa? (*Italian.*) Medusa. (*Her.*) Medusa? Turns out they're little jellyfish. "Then you won't catch me going in the water!" I says to him. And thus follows a giggly conversation about urinating on jellyfish stings and then I had to explain to him the phrase 'old wives tale'.

And I thought, a mini Med cruise, that'd be nice. That's the sort of thing people like us do when the kids are away. But we don't take holidays, we haven't since the disaster of Butlins, Bognor Regis in 1991. We can't bear to up sticks when she's in here. So we do a lot of gardening when we've the chance. There's a big hive of bees under the decking out the back. They're ginormous, these bees, they're like the cuddly pandas of the insect world. They started off in the drill holes for the cavity wall insulation and now they've taken over the decking. "Let them have it", I said to the husband, "I like the sound." They can barely fit between the wooden slats, they bump around trying to squeeze their chubby bodies through: they call that the 'waggle dance', don't they? Showing the others where to get the best pollen? Then down they go, through to their queen in the dark beneath our sun-loungers. We're in the habit of letting the grass grow for clover, I think the neighbours think we're a right pair of lazy sods. I sit out there with them at night, listening to the low hum of their work beneath the slats. We've, ah, we've always been prepared for old age – since our girl was four, I'd say – we had to live in a biddy bungalow with wide doors, bars in the bathroom. The three of us in our granny flat. Silly thought but when we had her I thought of my body like it was our garden - for her to play in, and on. She swam in it, swung off it, and I wanted it to be hers. Her, a great big panda-bee, and me her garden. You know apparently Albert Einstein said, 'if all the bees in the world disappear from the surface of the earth, man would have no more than four years to live'. There's one theory that our mobile phone towers and radiations have interfered with them being able to navigate around. Another theory says everyone but Scotland's got this nasty parasitic mite that's attacking the wild hives. Lucky Scotland, bloody typical they don't have our problems! You don't get parasites when you've got that much heather and socialism.

So we were given this wheelchair-adapted car in 1996. It was hell to park, and I called it the 'Bus', I bloody hated it! You could get a Motability vehicle back then, when the scheme was extended by the then Conservative government to include people with learning disabilities.

Ironically, the assessment for mobility allowance was also 'For Life' – due to the fact there's no prospect of her condition ever 'improving'. Now that's all been taken away, my daughter can't say 'I want to go and see my Mum and Dad in their biddy bungalow – "I'll pop out shall I? I'll get on a train, or wait for the bus?"

You see, after that bloody bus was taken back it suddenly became too upsetting for us to visit her – because we could no longer take her out with us. She'd howl for days afterwards, unable to be left, hating being stuck in there and watching us go, and the girls in here would ring and say she was 'uncontrollably upset.' And would we mind not coming til a week Tuesday. And we're obviously out of our minds about this. We can't even see our daughter cos it's too upsetting? What's better, our seeing her, and upsetting her – or – not seeing her at all? This was the conundrum. Our biggest joy used to be driving her home for the day, visiting her Grans on Saturdays, her cousins – the liberation that came with me buckling her in, suckering the SatNav to the windscreen and driving off with music blaring like we'd busted her out! But not now.

We decided – the only solution was to orphan her, to come in a disguise so that we could still see her. Honestly we felt like a right pair of knob-ends in this get-up – "Oh I see Mrs Clown's de-icing her windscreen again". But we're used to stares – if anything we've become quite the exhibitionists over the years. Besides we're all she's got. Because my family don't much like to visit hospitals. And now she's taken a turn for the worse – they don't want to hear how my daughter smells of death a bit. They think a parent should never have to smell that after the nappy years! How she's given up. How she gets thrush and cystitis from the catheter. How she gets pustules around her bum from lying about in a nappy all day. How she is liquid-fed through a PEG hole in her stomach and can't swallow solids. How her limbs have wasted, and the joints ache, how she gets cankles from water retention and how she has to wear Velcro slippers like her Gran! How she screams. How they have started putting anti-depressants in with her liquid feed.

I said to my husband last week – there's a double standard in there somewhere, because if she was a boy instead I'd probably get her a sex worker if she wanted one. And the husband said "Don't even think about it! Face it Linda, anyone who wants to sleep with our daughter's a pervert!" and we got into one heck of a row! The things we talk about! I said "What, just because she's a woman there's a finer line between abuse and liberation? She's a very sexual young woman actually!" And if she ever, ever said "Mum I'd quite like to have sex with someone" I'd be dialing a gigolo make no mistake! But that's why I gave her the vibrator, he didn't see it, he didn't see her touching herself! I know I shouldn't say these taboo things but how can I, her Mum, live with the knowledge of a million things she'll never have, places now she'll never go and I can't even help her have an orgasm?!

If she did meet someone I'd be yelling (*She puts her hand out palm up and waggles her fingers to mime stimulating a vagina.*) "For god's sake show him how to feed the pony! And for god's sake don't fake it, or some other poor bugger will inherit him!" I'd be all "Never sleep with a man unless he can make you come first!" – prior to entry as it were! Yes I'm very vocal – my husband's now an impeccable lover, poor sod. These days you can't get me off the top!

The husband joins us three times a week as Clown Number Two and on weekends he and I sit in the art room making papier-mache pigs and encouraging the kids with their physio. Because we no longer belong to our daughter. We've become the hospital clowns, property of all, parents of none. We just come along and help out. Make teas, clean up spills, find bits of jigsaw. You get on with it. I don't want to sound like a martyr. Because really, I can still watch her out the corner of my eye. Sometimes I think I see a hint of recognition in her eyes, but most days it's a cold stare, like I'm a complete stranger. She hasn't asked for us, she's grown calmer, she's not hurting herself any more. Because bloody hell, the last time she saw us in the flesh she tore out chunks of her hair, she bit the care assistants, she bit her own mouth until her lips bled, she tore at her t-shirt until it was just the neckline hanging by a thread, and then she grabbed a hairbrush and tried to scratch her eyes out!

Anyway this is the miracle: after we started coming in disguise, I bought her the first vibrator, and as I was the one visiting her most nights as Clown, well – I started to see the correlation. And the correlation was – that after she had – well my nephew would say 'rubbed one out' – She can speak! Quite normally! For just a minute! Only – how do I put it? How do I say to the physio and the OT – "Oh, I've noticed when she's a bit flushed, or when she's had her hand under the duvet she can speak! Speak with a real, a proper! – She makes sense! – there's real clarity!" How does a Mum say that? But I had to – find a way – to tell them this. Because I arrived one day after she'd used the little red 'Corsa' and that's when she looked me straight in the eye and said: "Thank you Clown." Her speech wasn't incoherent, slurred, noises, out came a tirade of beautiful clear words, all brilliantly clear and formed in her mouth. She hasn't spoken, ever! She's made nothing but noises her entire life! Now she makes little observations, asks someone to brush her hair, open the window, name a bird, pick a flower she's spotted out the window. But whatever she says, really, for those few minutes – I think, and I'm biased, but it's the most beautiful, if you like, the most *profound* thing I've ever heard in all my life. No, I am biased because also – see I didn't know what her voice would sound like and she's got my accent, to a T! She's got mine! A right gob on her!

And so – it troubled me at first, but then the doctors thought this was a real scientific find, and so I thought maybe I've done the right thing, a good thing – I've given her something to make up for this – I had a small hand in a miracle, giving her a bit of pleasure back – and so our doctors were at a neuroscience conference and suddenly Doctor Salvatore is coming over. And even though we've built up a rapport, and he seems lovely – I had a thought and the thought was – what if I die and my husband dies and they come and do tests on her like she's an animal? Like those horrid sanatoriums in the 1800s. What if they put her in a thin white chemise and take photos of her in her raptures?

Or put her in restraints, wheel her off and my family do nothing – What if they insert probes or electrodes what if – because I don't trust this world to look out for her – and for – for all his Latin charm, what if we're not here to watch over her and they stop treating her as a human being – now it's not that I don't trust the Italians. They're wonderful, sensual people! But they had a very different war to us didn't they.

I don't trust them to look out for her! What will happen when we die? I knew what was coming. I wrote to them all. I received a very impersonal, printed postcard from the prime minister's office, informing me that "my concerns had been passed on to the relevant authorities", and an automated email telling me that the ministers were "too busy to deal with my comments in person". I've printed that out.

But I can't be angry with their cowardice. I'm just sad, I'm sad and I'm scared! Sad that they targeted the most vulnerable in our "big society" – those of us who can't defend ourselves! But to – you might say – *intellectualise* it, even to speak of it now as I am, is just *us*, 'the able', talking about those who can't speak. Or who can only speak for a few minutes! To say this now is to give the argument back to the able! So who can speak for them? Cos I bloody will! I want all the things she doesn't think to ask for! I'll speak! Because why should my girl ever, ever, have to ask for a basic human right? To have enough benefit money for toiletries and a good supply of AA batteries! (*She winks.*) And a scheme that rents us a car, and services her wheelchair, and lets her leave this bloody place and drive out with her silly old Mum and Dad? What a sight we must be.

(*She puts on the red nose.*)

Thankfully no one asks for balloon animals or ought tricky – I'm not very creative – but we just sort of mess about and do bad mimes and it's probably a bit like Christmas charades at ours, only with less brandy.

(*She puts on his hi-vis tabard.*)

I nicked this from my husband because he can never get away at the end of the week – he's a foreman – so now Friday's clown is 'Glow Clown.' Apparently I'm actually helping everyone with their Days of the Week. So I'm off to entertain my orphans. Who will do this when I'm really dead? Who will tell her I did this? I've said to the husband, "Bury me in my wig, full make up." And I want 'Loving Mother and Amateur Clown' on my headstone. (*She laughs.*)

(*She readies herself, straightens up, fixes a smile.*)

I hope he did say that, Einstein. He sounded like a nice man. He sounded like – well anyone who thinks about the little things, like protecting bees, in the bigger picture – they sound like the kind of person I'd rather have running the country. Cos we're supposed to believe that *they're* the experts on the world, these men who stand up, safe on their stages. Not the beekeepers and the scientists and the Mums. We've got to swallow it: that what *they* say is a priority, or an expense, is gospel. That we're the little people, that we're not to add our tuppence-worth. We *are* little people. I'm not going to write theories that change the world, discover new life forms or anything now; but I don't see them polishing their Nobel Prizes either! And I know they're wrong. I *know* it. Because the little I do know about relativity is this: if those coalition men came on down to this care home and watched me perform they'd see that we have the same laws of physics operating on us. Afterwards I'd crack out the custard creams for them and we'd sit down and have a nice civilised tea. I'd start off with a bit of cheek, I'd say, "After what you've started, I hope your wives are no longer giving you blow jobs!" And then I'd say: "But you and me boys, we're the same aren't we? Or do you have more gravity operating on you when you have power and privilege, does it take more to weigh you down when your pockets are filled with money?" I'd tell them about cognitive neuroscience and kinaesthetic empathy, and Doctor Salvatore, and I'd remind them that our mirror neurons were firing right that second. I'd point to my girl in the corner and I'd be quite chipper, I'd say – "I was a Mother once. That girl over there's my flesh and blood. (*She taps her own chest.*) And then I'd just take hold of their hands, and I'd say "And this – this is flesh too – this is flesh, and it bleeds."

(*Peering in the door.*)

There we are – there's my cue – a hush has fallen – and for effect – they're a good lot in here.

See – they turn the lights out before I go on.

(*She takes a deep breath. Exhales. She exits through the door. Many screams and shouts offstage as she enters the communal room. The door slams behind her.*)

The End.

Other collections from Oberon Books

The Great Game: Afghanistan

Features plays by: Colin Teevan, Richard Bean, David Greer, Ron Hutchinson, Naomi Wallace, Lee Blessing, David Edgar, Amit Gupta, Stephen Jeffreys, Ben Ockrent, Simon Stephens, Joy Wilkinson

The Great Game: Afghanistan is an extraordinary cycle of short plays, written by some of Britain's leading contemporary playwrights, which attempt to broaden our understanding of the explosive history of western involvement in Afghanistan.

£14.99 / 9781840029222

Hidden Gems

These distinctive new volumes of drama by black British playwrights exemplify how experiments with form, subject matter and genre can serve to centralise the experiences of black people in local, national and international contexts of culture, politics and performance. Each play is critically introduced, to create an anthology of interactions – between the people who have long championed the work through teaching and writing about it and the people who produce, perform and explain their intentions behind it.

Hidden Gems: Volume One Edited by Deirdre Osborne
Features plays:
B is for Black by Courttia Newland
Moj of the Antartic by Mojisola Adebayo
The Sons of Charlie Paora by Lennie James
Brown Girl in the Ring by Valerie Mason-John
Something Dark by Lemn Sissay
35 Cents by Paul Anthony Morris
£14.99 / 9781840028430

Hidden Gems: Volume Two Edited by Deirdre Osborne
Features plays:
A Bitter Herb by Kwame Kwei-Armah
The Far Side by Courttia Newland
Identity by Paul Antony Morris
Mary Seacole by SuAndi
Absolution by Malika Booker
Urban Afro-Saxons by Patricia Eldridge and Kofi Ageyomi
£14.99 / 9781849430111

For more collections and anthologies from Oberon Books visit
www.oberonbooks/collections.html

Follow us on www.twitter.com/@oberonbooks
& www.facebook.com/oberonbook

Other writing from Theatre Uncut authors published by Oberon Books

The Suspect Culture Book

Edited by Graham Eatough & Dan Rebellato
with contributions from David Greig

Suspect Culture was Scotland's leading experimental theatre company between 1993 and 2009. Based in Glasgow, it was formed of a core group of associate artists who collaborated in making groundbreaking, high quality new work which gained an international reputation.

This book surveys the company's history and ideas and includes an overview of the company by David Greig; co-founder, writer, dramaturg and sometime actor with Suspect Culture and the perspective of Brazilian director and writer Mauricio Paroni de Castro, one of Suspect Culture's many international atrocities associates. Also included here are the previously unpublished playtexts of three of its most celebrated shows, *Timeless, Mainstream* and *Lament* (all created by the company with text by David Greig).

£14.99 / 9781849430876

Dennis Kelly: Plays One

The four plays in this first collection by Dennis Kelly are linked by their characters' desperate need to believe that there is more to life than the often brutal worlds in which they find themselves.
Features the plays *Debris, Osama the Hero, After the End* and *Love and Money*.

£14.99 / 9781840028034

Single Editions from Oberon Books

Bud Take the Wheel, I Feel a Song Coming On by Clara Brennan
£9.99 / 9781849430760

After the End by Dennis Kelly
£7.99 / 9781840025804

DNA by Dennis Kelly
£8.99 / 9781840028409

Debris by Dennis Kelly
£9.99 / 9781840024333

Love and Money by Dennis Kelly
£8.99 / 9781840026955

Orphans by Dennis Kelly
£8.99 / 9781840029437

Osama the Hero by Dennis Kelly
£7.99 / 9781840025743

Taking Care of Baby by Dennis Kelly
£8.99 / 9781840027785

To order any of the above books, please contact:
Marston Books, PO Box 269, Abingdon, Oxon, OX14 4YN
Email: direct.orders@marston.co.uk / Telephone: 01234 465577, Fax: 01235 465556

Or visit www.oberonbooks.com